OTHERS LORD

A Snapshot of the Life
and Legacy of
Lorine C. McLeod

SPENCER L. DUFFY

Foreword by Dr. John D. Fuller,
Sr., Pastor, Lewis Chapel Missionary Baptist Church

Silver Spring, Maryland

Copyright (c) 2015 Spencer Duffy

All rights reserved. Printed in the U.S.A.

No part of this publication may be reproduced or transmitted in any form or by any means, electronic or mechanical, including photocopy, recording or any information storage and retrieval system now known or to be invented, without permission in writing from the publisher, except by a reviewer who wishes to quote brief passages in connection with a review written for inclusion in a magazine, newspaper or broadcast.

Published in the United States by
Beckham Publications Group, Inc.
P.O. Box 4066, Silver Spring, MD 20914
ISBN: 978-0-9905904-3-9
Library of Congress Cataloging in Publication:

Table of Contents

Foreword...............................v

Acknowledgments......................vii

1. Lorine's Eary Years..................1

Photos Inset..........................9

2. Lorine's Caring Nature.............29

3. I Love Thy Church, O God..........31

4. Gone Fishing......................33

5. Her Time with the Tent............35

References..........................39

Foreword

I am honored to write these words on behalf of Lorine Cole McLeod, a dedicated and faithful servant of God. I met Mrs. McLeod at a time when her church was seeking a pastor. She was in the forefront of leading the congregation to elect someone who would lead the church from part-time to full-time ministry.

For almost forty-two years under my leadership, she has been the one constant individual who never wavered from doing what was best for her church, family, community, and God.

I hope this snapshot of her life will bring inspiration, encouragement, and joy to you, the reader.

Dr. John D. Fuller, Sr., Pastor
Lewis Chapel Missionary Baptist Church
Fayetteville, North Carolina

Acknowledgments

I am eternally grateful to Ms. Delores Henderson for typing and electronically transmitting the manuscript to the publisher, to Rev. Sr. Anita M. Forde for her professional editing of this book, to my loving wife, Barbara, who designed the artwork for the cover and for the collage, and finally to God our creator who allows good people like Lorine C. McLeod to bless and enrich our lives.

CHAPTER 1

Lorine's Early Years

Lorine was born November 4, 1921, in a little village called Duffy's Station on the outer skirts of Fayetteville, North Carolina. She is the sixth of eight siblings born from the union of Alexander Cole and Rosella Patterson Cole. Six of the eight children were boys: Hubbard, James, CharlesEdward, Willie, Alexander and Clifton. The girls were Marie and Lorine. Lorine was several years older than her sister, Marie, so she spent more of her growing up time with her brothers. She grew up on a farm in Hoke County, North Carolina. Her father was a sharecropper. This was a common type of tenant farming where the landlord provided the house and the money to start the crop and the tenant provided the labor to bring the crop from seed to harvest. Under the sharecropping system, the landlord had complete control of the finances and was sole keeper of the record of expenditures and returns from the harvest. Therefore, the tenant farmer had to take the landlord's word as to whether the harvest returned a profit. If it did, the profit was shared between the landlord and the tenant farmer. If not, the tenant farmer got little or no money from that year's harvest. Lorine and her family worked hard on the farm hoping to make a good crop and get some money from the harvest. From an early age, Lorine showed her ability and willingness to learn. She not only learned to hoe and pick cotton but also to sucker and harvest tobacco. Positioned by birth between two boys, she even learned to plow which was a chore that was usually left for the boys.

Of the two crops, cotton and tobacco, the latter was the more profitable because it paid more per pound at the marketplace. Consequently, a better tobacco crop meant a better chance of making a

1

profit and getting some money at harvesttime. While Lorine's father knew how to grow high quality tobacco—from the seedling stage to the harvesting and curing stage, Lorine found tobacco more challenging to grow than cotton. By contrast, it had several more steps in its development than cotton. It had to be suckered (removing the tiny shoots that grew between the leaf and the stem). These suckers were sticky and had a pungent odor that Lorine found unbearable. On many occasions, she would leave the field sick from the odor of the suckers only to return the next day to continue until all of the suckers were removed. Additionally, tobacco had to be harvested at the appropriate time, strung and cured in a smokehouse before taking it to the market. On the other hand, while cotton was also laborious, after chopping (hoeing out the weeds), no other work was required from the laborers until harvesting. Harvesting cotton was backbreaking because of the short height of the cotton plants. The cotton sacks were heavy when filled and plucking the cotton from the sharp bowls was hard on one's fingers. Notwithstanding the drudgery of farming, Lorine showed her will and determination to succeed at any task set before her.

Lorine remembered one year following a good harvest of cotton and tobacco that she accompanied her sister in law to town where she selected a winter coat that she really liked and hoped to purchase from earnings from that year's harvest. She was confident that that year's crop would have yielded a profit and that there would have been adequate money to purchase the coat that she had selected. However, when her father went to the landlord to "settle up" (a term used by farmers in determining the profit or loss from the year's harvest), the landlord told her father that the cost of growing the crops equalled the profit. As a result, there was no profit, and consequently, there was no money for them that year. To Lorine, that was indeed a terrible blow. She believed that the landlord had cheated them and had kept all of the profits for himself. That incident turned Lorine against farming and she swore that as soon as she graduated from school she would leave the farm. Shortly after that incident, Lorine and her family moved to another farm in Hoke County nearby a place called Rock Fish that was approximately three miles from White Oak. While living there, Lorine attended Lewis Chapel Elementary School and lived with her eldest brother, Hubbard, and his family.

Sometime later, Lorine's father moved the family to Cumberland County near Fayetteville, North Carolina, where Lorine was enrolled in White Oak Elementary School. Now Lorine's brothers were very athletic. In fact, they were particularly good at baseball. Once more because of her positioning by birth, Lorine learned to play ball with them. She not only became an excellent pitcher but also made the team on the White Oak School Girls' Softball Team. It was her latter skill in softball that got her in trouble with her father. Lorine's father observed very strict rules with regards to the time that his children got home: they, particularly the girls, had to be home before dark. Lorine had become the number one pitcher for the White Oak School's Softball Team and her team was the most winning team in Cumberland County. However, there was a rival team from another school that gave White Oak a run for its money. Near the end of the softball season, Lorine's team and the rival team were neck in neck for the championship. Although the rival team had lost the last game played against White Oak, it was determined to get its revenge by defeating White Oak in the championship game. On the other hand, White Oak was equally determined not to be defeated and to take home the championship.

There was a winning strategy that the White Oak's coach had and he discussed it with Lorine whom he not only saw as his best pitcher but also wanted to start the game. Ball games were played after school and usually ended before sundown thus enabling the students to get home before dark. Mention was made in the previous paragraph of the strict rules that Lorine's father had in effect regarding the time that his children, particularly the girls, were home from school. In the light of these rules, Lorine told her father about the game and asked his permission to stay late. Reluctantly, he agreed but sternly admonished her to be home before dark. After school that day, the big game was on. Everybody was excited. The rival team looked sharp and ready to go. Lorine, fearing that the game would run into overtime asked her coach, who did not have a car, to ask the rival coach to take her home if the game ran into overtime. The request was made, and the rival coach agreed following which the game commenced. Lorine was pitching up a storm. The game got tied up, and the coach put in his number two pitcher in order to give Lorine some rest. The number two pitcher gave up a couple of runs thus putting White Oak behind. Consequently, the coach put Lorine back in the game, and the battle raged on. It was in the ninth ending when once more the game got tied up. By that time, it was not only getting late but also the game was going into overtime. Lorine reminded her coach that she had to be home before dark. He assured her of a ride home and begged her to stay and pitch the overtime ending. The competing team came to bat and managed to get two players on base; however, because of Lorine's superior pitching the rival team could not score. Next, it was White Oak's turn to bat. The sun was just above the treetops, and the first girl at the plate hit a home run winning the game. Lorine scarcely had time to savor the victory. Her coach was overjoyed and congratulated her for her fine pitching but in the same breath told her that the rival coach could not take her home because he had some of his players who were under the same restrictions to which she was subject and he had to take them home.

Having received that bad news from her coach, Lorine struck out running by which time it was dusk dark and she was approximately three miles from her home. She ran until she was breathless and then walked until she regained enough strength to resume her running. On approaching the vicinity of the woods, between the school and her home, she saw two of her brothers who were coming to meet her. Immediately, she burst into tears because she knew that her father had sent them to look for her. Before she could say anything to them, one of her brothers asked her the reason for staying at school so late when she knew that their father would be terribly upset. She, truthfully gave them the reason. Her brothers understood but knew, however, that that reason would not satisfy their father. When they arrived home, it was dark and their father was waiting angrily. Before Lorine could say anything to him, he ordered her brothers to go to the woods and get him several good switches. Those switches he platted together and instructed Lorine to go to the other room and remove all of her clothes. He entered the room, beat her unmercifully, and then left the room without a word. That flogging left Lorine with welts and contusions from her neck to her buttocks. While Lorine realized that she had broken her father's rule, she could neither understand nor accept the severe beating that he had given her. In addition, although this was the worst beating that her father had given her, it did not tarnish her love and respect for him. Shortly after that incident, he fell ill, and she became his main caregiver. While he neither mentioned nor commented on that beating, he seemed to be overly nice to her. He developed a scalp condition that caused him severe itching. He would call on her to scratch his head to relieve the itching. After she finished, he would thank her and tell her how good it felt. As part of his illness, he developed kidney trouble and succumbed to the disease. Although Lorine loved her father, it was not until after his death that she found it in her heart to forgive him for that, by far, her worst beating.

After Lorine's father died, the maid who worked for the landlord overheard him say that he would take all of Lorine's family possessions, including the corn that they had in the barn, because of the mountain of debt that they had incurred during the father's illness. Consequently,

with a neighbor's assistance, the family packed up and slipped away by night to another farm. That farm was in close proximity to Chestnut High School and it became the high school that Lorine attended. While attending Chestnut High School, Lorine became interested in boys. It was customary then for several boys in the neighborhood to meet the girls as they walked home from school. One young man named James (nicknamed Little Boy) started talking to Lorine and before long they were courting and he asked Lorine if he could visit her at her home. Lorine did not allow him because her mother thought that she was too young to have such company at her home. Nevertheless, Little Boy was persistent and as often as he could, he would meet Lorine on her way home from school. They liked each other a lot. So they decided to be girlfriend and boyfriend. By the time the friendship became serious, Lorine was old enough to receive company at her home. For Little Boy, that was a cherished moment! He was anxious to meet Lorine's mother and seek her approval for their courtship. Lorine was then in the tenth grade. Little Boy popped the question! ... He asked her to marry him. Lorine said no because she had promised her mother that she would not get married before she finished high school. Little Boy, without too much thought, said, "Well, I'll wait."

Little Boy was pretty popular with the girls. Although Lorine held the best hand, there were other girls pursuing him. Actually, unbeknown to Lorine, Little Boy had been seeing at least one other girl who felt that she was in a relatively close relationship with him. It was by accident or better by incident that Lorine found out about that girl … . Little Boy had purchased a fancy classic wristwatch and asked Lorine if she would have liked to wear it to school that day, to which Lorine said, "Yes, of course!". Little did she know that Little Boy had shown his watch to the other girl, who confronted Lorine when she saw her wearing the watch. She attempted to take the watch off of Lorine's wrist, and the fight was on. This landed them both in the principal's office. After the principal questioned them both about the altercation, he took the watch and told them that he would return it only after deciding who should have it and what their punishment for misbehaving would be. The principal's position, put Lorine on the spot. She pondered over how she would tell Little Boy all of what happened. At the same time, she studied how she would let him know that she did not appreciate his seeing other girls particularly since they were engaged. The very next day as Little Boy walked Lorine home from school, he noticed that she was not wearing his watch and he asked her about it. She told him of the fight, the principal's decision and that she did not appreciate him seeing other girls while they were engaged to marry. Surprisingly, Little Boy took it better than she expected. Fortunately, for Lorine, the principal returned the watch to her and required that she and the other girl stay after school and perform extra work in his office.

After high school, Lorine wanted to attend college and was prepared to ask Little Boy to wait for four more years. Her choice was Hampton University having been inspired by one of her teachers who was a graduate of Hampton. She liked the way that teacher carried herself with dignity, poise and steadfast professionalism. Additionally, the teacher encouraged her by letting her know that she could arrange for her to stay with her sister who not only lived in Norfolk but also provided lodging for college students. As it turned out, Lorine's family was struggling financially, and there was no money for her to attend Hampton. Consequently, shortly after Lorine graduated from Chestnut High School, she and Little Boy got married.

At first, the happy couple lived with Lorine's motherinlaw. The landlord saw the benefit of having a young couple to assist on the farm. Consequently, he built a small cottage adjacent to Lorine's motherin-law's house, and it was there that the newlyweds started as husband and wife. They were not only happy to have their own place but also pleased to work with that landlord who had shown them such favor. For several years, James and Lorine farmed with her mother-in-law. Even after her motherinlaw fell ill and moved away to live with her sister, James and Lorine stayed and continued to farm at the same location. However, although they raised good crops, having to hire laborers to assist with the cultivating and harvesting cut deep into the profits. As a result, they often got little or no money from a whole year of hard work and before long they gave up farming and moved to the nearby city of Fayetteville. It did not take long for Lorine to find work in the city. She started working in a dry cleaning shop, and as with her school work, she was a quick learner. She learned to press clothes, and the shop manager, quickly observing her potential, promoted her to the position of head presser. The business did well and thrived because Lorine turned out superbly pressed garments and customer loyalty was a hallmark of the business. Lorine became known as one of the best pressers in Fayetteville and for many years worked at that shop. Finally, one day she had a dispute with the owner and decided to quit. Shortly after leaving, she found work as a presser in another shop. She had worked only a few weeks in the new shop when to her astonishment she saw her former boss standing in the doorway and he quietly beckoned to her to come to him. Indeed, he was reluctant to enter the shop and talk to her because he was on his competitor's property. At first, Lorine ignored him. Finally, she conceded to see what he wanted .... He promised her good treatment and a substantial raise if she would return to his employ. Lorine found his offer agreeable and finished her pressing career at his shop.

Lorine's husband also found work in Fayetteville. What a happy and excited couple they were with their new start in Fayetteville! After World War II, Fort Bragg put a number of Officers' Quarters housing up for sale. The couple purchased one of the units and had it moved to Robertson Street Extended. It was there that they lived until James passed and for many years after his passing Lorine lived there until a developer looked at the community and decided that he wanted the entire area to build a golf course and a housing complex. He offered to build Lorine a new house in another part of town; however, she refused his offer. She told him that she wanted to remain in the house that she and her late husband had purchased shortly after they got married. The developer agreed to find a place in Fayetteville to Lorine's liking and move her house to that location. They agreed on a lot on Ellis Street and her house was moved to the present address—720 Ellis Street. Furthermore, the developer provided considerable improvements to the house including a new roof, siding and an interior paint job.

Photos | 9

Relaxing while fishing

At church

10 | Others Lord

Banquet

More advising

Photos | 11

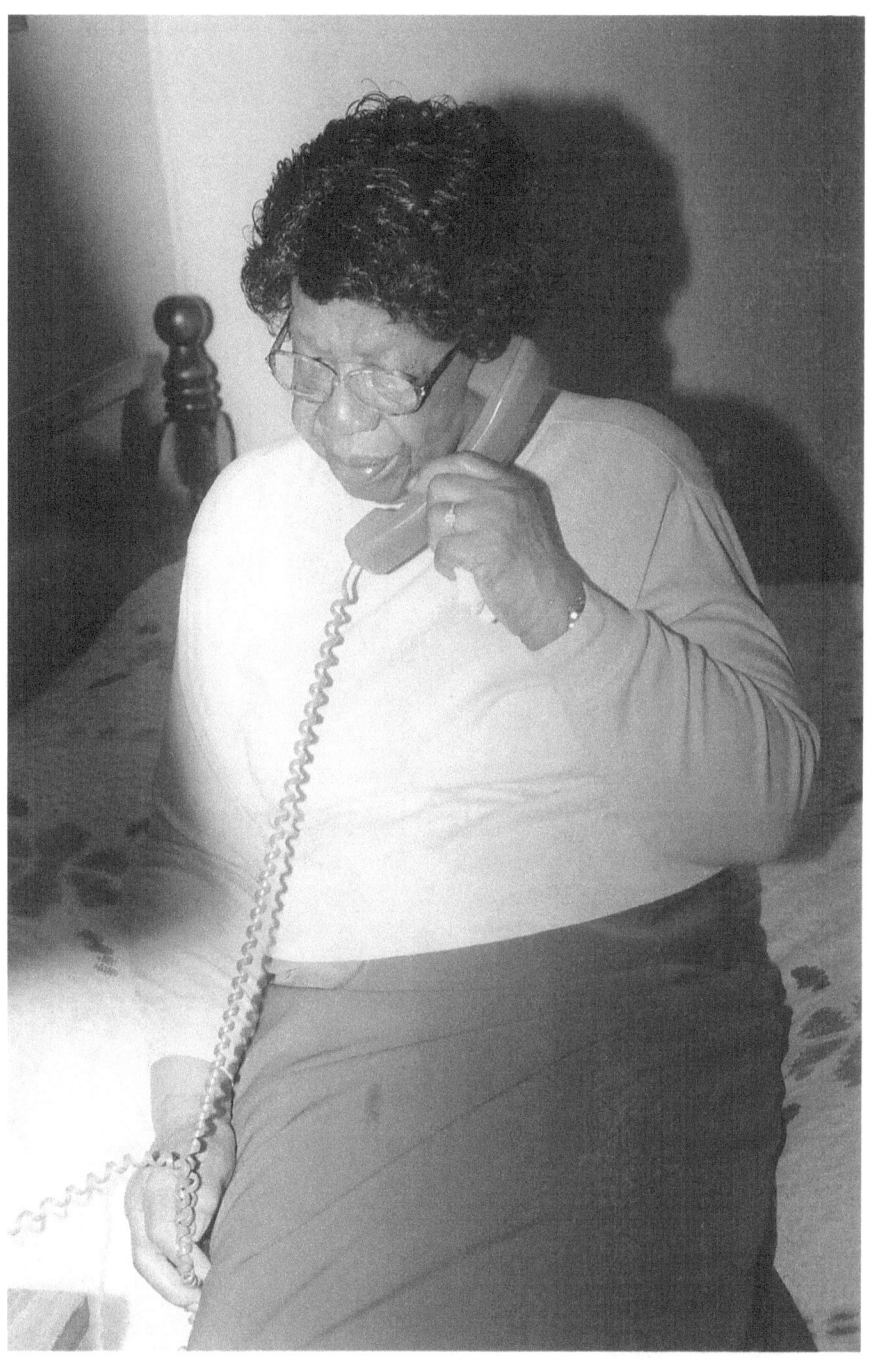

Phone conference

12 | Others Lord

Celebration

With friends

Photos | 13

McLeod and then vice president

President McLeod and Rev. John D. Fuller

McLeod with banner showing original Tent name

Happily mobile

Current president
Lodies Jackson Glosten

Diane Newell

Photos | 15

Mary Rambert, caregiver

Pam Gayle, caregiver

16 | Others Lord

Annis Graham, caregiver; worked with caregiver Clarissa Norman, photo missing

Early Tents convention

Photos | 17

A Tent convention

A Tent convention

18 | Others Lord

Banquet

Retirement cake

Photos | 19

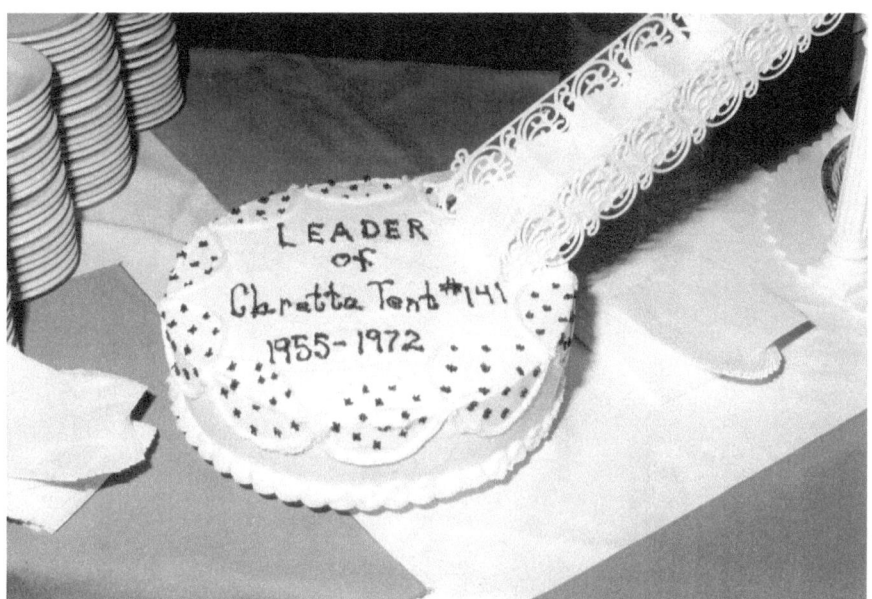

Anniversary cake Claratta Tent #141

A celebration

Honorary plaques

Lorine C. McLeod Tent Hall

Tent Hall entrance

Tent Hall, side view

Family members outside Lewis Chapel Missionary Baptist Church, Rev. Dr. John D. Fuller, Sr., pastor;
l to r, Barbara Duffy; Bryan Cole; Helen Cole; Lorine McLeod; Clifton Cole; Keith Cole; Mary Cole

Bullock McLeod Apartments groundbreaking ceremony

Photos | 23

White Oak Elementary School site

Gospel Choir President, 26 years [1975]

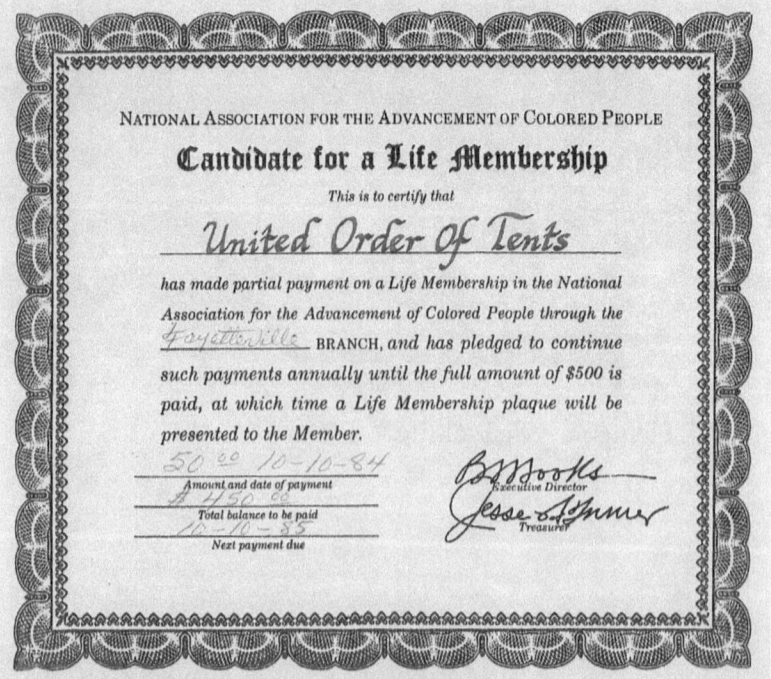

NAACP Life Membership Candidate [1984]

Photos | 25

BOB ETHERIDGE
2ND DISTRICT, NORTH CAROLINA

COMMITTEE ON WAYS AND MEANS
  SUBCOMMITTEE ON TRADE
  SUBCOMMITTEE ON OVERSIGHT

COMMITTEE ON THE BUDGET

SENIOR WHIP

WASHINGTON, DC 20515
(202) 225-4531

DISTRICT OFFICES:
333 FAYETTEVILLE STREET, SUITE 5(
RALEIGH, NC 27601
(919) 829-9122
1 (888) 262-6202

P.O. Box 1059
609 NORTH 1ST STREET
LILLINGTON, NC 27546
(910) 814-0335
1 (866) 384-3743

www.house.gov/etheridge

Congress of the United States
House of Representatives
Washington, DC 20515

May 22, 2010

Dr. Lorine Cole McLeod
731 Ellis Street
Fayetteville, North Carolina 28301

Dear Dr. McLeod:

It is my privilege to extend greetings and sincere congratulations to you as your members, family and friends celebrate the Sojourner Truth Tent #770 25th Anniversary on May 22, 2010. It is my understanding that you have played a major role in the United Order of Tents Southern District # 1 for over sixty years. I was told that during the past 20 years you have served as a "Tent Leader, Deputy and President of this 142 year old organization.

This special event will provide an avenue for tent members, family and friends to pay tribute to you for your unwavering devotion and leadership. Over the years, you have worked tirelessly to make a positive difference in our state and nation. Please take this opportunity to look back with pride on your many years of service that have positively impacted the lives of countless citizens. I know that you will continue to serve as a strong voice for the poor and disadvantaged and we pause today to say thank you.

You are to be commended for a job well done. On behalf of the residents of the 2nd Congressional District, we send our best wishes for your continued success.

Sincerely,

Bob Etheridge
Member of Congress

Congressman Etheridge greetings [2010]

Church study course completion [1997]

Shaw Divinity School Doctor of
Christian Letters honoris causa [1988]

Photos | 27

General Baptist State Convention of North Carolina, Inc. Presidential Award [2003]

North Carolina Conference of Tents recognition [1995]

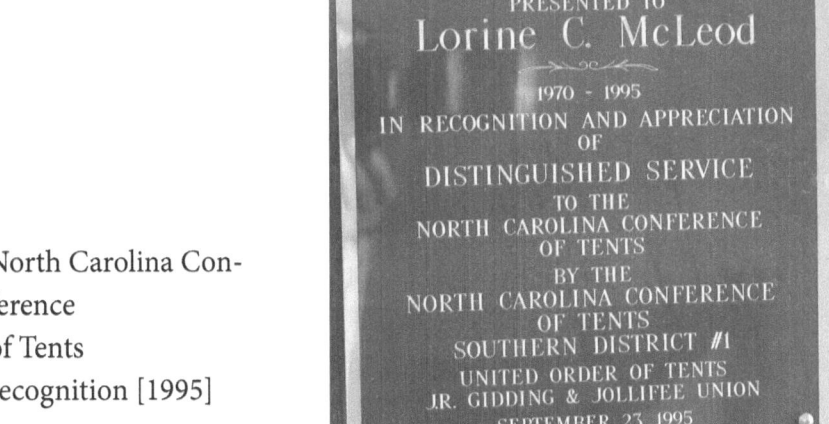

CHAPTER 2

Lorine's Caring Nature

Although Lorine had no biological children, she loved her family, particularly her nieces and nephews. She was always in contact with them and came to their rescue whenever they needed her. They could always rely on their Aunt Lorine to look out for them. One niece, Barbara, was special! Even before Lorine got married and while she was a teenager at Chestnut High School, she would pick Barbara up on her way from school and take her home with her. Sometimes it would be cold and Lorine would get a blanket or a gently used coat to wrap Barbara in for the long walk between Chestnut High School and her house. When Barbara became old enough to go to school, Lorine would visit the school regularly. Many summers after school was out, Lorine would have Barbara spend the summers at her home. She was like a second mother to Barbara and a special aunt to all of her nieces and nephews. Lorine's loving and caring nature for the young extended beyond her immediate family. Many of the younger women at her church, Lewis Chapel Missionary Baptist, still greet her as Mother McLeod. She has a way of making young people feel appreciated and loved and they are always happy to be in her presence.

CHAPTER 3

I Love Thy Church, O God

Lorine joined Lewis Chapel Missionary Baptist Church in 1937 under the pastorship of Rev. R. L. Carr. The Church was then called Lewis Chapel Baptist Church. When she joined, Lewis Chapel was a small frame church with a membership of less than 200 worshippers. USA Churches in its directory would classify the church as medium in size with an average weekend attendance between 51 and 300 persons. According to the USA Churches' Directory, "Church size does not refer to the physical size of the church building or the number of seats in the church building, or even the number of people who are members of the church." In 1973, Lorine and her husband, James, formed a committee to search for a new pastor. They found a young minister named John D. Fuller who was 27 years old when he was chosen to be the pastor. He went to Lewis Chapel with a vision of serving the Fayetteville community and building a larger facility on the existing site. Lorine and her husband shared the pastor's vision and the three began working to make the vision a reality. Rev. Fuller launched a door-to-door campaign in which he invited people (particularly the young) not only to worship at but also to join Lewis Chapel. The Church membership began to increase and before long the small frame church was filled to capacity and it was obvious that its expansion was necessary. Although they had the land, they needed the plan and the money to construct a larger structure on the existing site. Lorine and her husband were instrumental in raising funds and encouraging the membership to cooperate in shouldering such a challenging task. While some of the members doubted whether they could raise enough money to demolish the existing structure and construct an edifice that would hold more than 2,000 people, Lorine never doubted. She and her husband worked tirelessly with Rev. Fuller who recognized Lorine's strong will and leadership abilities. Additionally, he saw in her a woman of great faith, one who could get things done without a lot of fanfare or confusion and one with the ability to have people listen when she spoke. They started a building fund, and in minimum time, they had accumulated enough money to break ground for the new sanctuary. Today, a modern edifice stands on the site. In the inner area of the sanctuary stands the Lorine C. McLeod Fellowship Hall: a testament to her service as a faithful member and a serious Christian worker at Lewis Chapel.

Lorine has served in many offices in Lewis Chapel: first female General Superintendent and Financial Secretary, President of the Union Baptist Association Women's Auxiliary, Bible instructor, Chairperson of the Scholarship Banquet, Chairperson, Executive Board member and President of the Daughters of Zion Middle District Association. Other positions of President were that of the Gospel Choir, Floral Club, Missionary Circle, and Pastor's Aid and Auxiliary.

For 50 years, she taught Sunday school and started the A1 Missionary Society at the Church. Numerous plaques, certificates and awards grace her living room walls in recognition of her leadership and service. Included are: Outstanding Alumni Award, Long Leaf Pine Award (the 9th highest civilian award in the State of North Carolina), General Baptist State Convention Award, Distinguished Service Award for North Carolina, Conference of Tents Award, and the Honorary Degree of Doctor of Christian Letters from Shaw University Divinity School. Although Lorine is now in her nineties, she still attends church business meetings and willingly shares her advice and wise counsel with the membership. Because of health challenges, Lorine is now confined to a wheelchair but that does not stop her ... . She attends church regularly, she is highly respected among the membership and is known as the Church Mother. A special place in the sanctuary is reserved for her.

CHAPTER 4

Gone Fishing

Although there were few opportunities for recreation in Lorine's busy life, she would not pass up an opportunity to go fishing. Whenever she had a chance, she would slip away to one of her favorite fishing spots which included piers off the coastal waters of North Carolina and Virginia. She especially enjoyed fishing with her brother, Al (Alexander), and her sister in law, Liz (Elizabeth). They would fish for many hours in both fresh and saltwater locations from Top Sail to James River, and the coastal waters at Myrtle Beach and Wilmington, Delaware. In addition, she found time to drop a hook in places less known, such as the Cape Fear River, creeks and unnamed ponds in the Fayetteville area. Her favorite lure to bait the hooks was earthworms.

She, her brother and her sister in law conducted many debates as to who was the best fisher. Although there was never a declared winner, Lorine knew that she was the best. Her biggest single catch was a flounder caught off the coast of Norfolk, Virginia. He struck her line with such ferocity that she thought that she had caught a small shark. The way he fought, she knew that she had snagged a big one! He tested her strength and endurance. With the help of her brother, it took almost 20 minutes to reel him in. When she finally landed him, he weighed in at 20 pounds. That was the prize catch for the day! Her biggest mass catch was off a pier in the Atlantic Ocean near Wilmington, Delaware shortly after Hurricane Hazel. She loved fishing because it gave her the opportunity to be out near the water in the fresh air and feel a sudden tug on her line. When she caught too many fish for her family, she gladly shared them with her friends.

CHAPTER 5

Her Time with the Tent

Lorine learned about the Tent Organization from her neighbor who had two daughters in that organization. At the time, the organization was on a recruitment campaign and the neighbor's daughters invited her to one of their meetings. Lorine asked about the Tent's mission and major purpose and they told her that the United Order of Tents was a women's only organization and the oldest African American female organization in the United States. Its mission was to support the sisterhood and to help those in the community who were in need. Lorine liked the structure and the mission of the organization, so she joined. Being an excited new member who wanted to learn all that she could about the organization, she conducted her own research. Consequently, she learned that the United Order of Tents was founded in 1867 by Annetta M. Lane with the assistance of her friend, Harriot Taylor. It was incorporated in Norfolk, Virginia in 1908. From an early age, Mrs. Lane became interested in freeing her sisters from slavery and participated in the Underground Railroad to the extent of giving her valuable coral bracelet to a ship's captain to pay for the passage of a black family to escape to freedom. She was a faithful member of Saint Paul A.M.E. Church for 58 years.

The current mission of the United Order of Tents is to look after its members, provide nursing care and a home for its infirm sisters, encourage the sisterhood to execute its voting rights and to energize women to attain the highest standard of Christian living. Included in its objective is the idea of "lifting as we climb", realizing that the race can rise no higher than the standards set by its women. To that end, juvenile classes aimed at combating juvenile delinquency and providing scholarships for deserving young women were established. The organization includes women from all walks of life. Neither status, prestige, wealth, nor religious affiliation is considered in determining eligibility for membership, and it has more than 100 chapters. Two Caucasian men from Ohio helped establish the organization by providing the money and the legal advice, free of charge, to get the organization started. In return, they asked that their names be included in the full name of the organization. Consequently, until this day, the full name of the United Order of Tents is the Jr. Gidding and Jollifee Union Order of Tents. The name 'Tent' was chosen for the organization because literally tents were the basic housing for early Christians and a place where runaway slaves would stop along the Underground Railroad as they made their way from slavery to freedom.

Inspired by the history and purpose of the Tent, Lorine became a member of the local chapter and immediately began to work in service to the sisterhood which, in turn, quickly saw her dedication and leadership abilities. Before long, she was elected president of the local chapter. That was only the beginning of a long chain of her achievements which led to her presidency of the United Order of Tent District, Number 1. This area included North Carolina, South Carolina, Virginia, Maryland and Washington, D.C. Under her presidency, the organization's membership grew from about 14,000 to approximately 20,000 active members. Lorine travelled the length and breadth of District 1 inspiring, motivating and encouraging her sisters to work in the service of the Tent and to strive to fulfill its mission.

During her tenure as president, the Tent Organization grew strong. It not only acquired land and built a senior citizens living complex and a headquarters office in Norfolk, Virginia but also grew financially. Lorine encouraged her members to sponsor profitable events and invest some of the money for financial stability and future programs. One of her signature fundraisers was the Four Seasons Dinner Banquet. This event presented foods relevant to each of the four seasons (Spring, Summer, Fall and Winter). Participating members would cook the appropriate foods for their respective season and sell tickets to their friends and the general public. The tables and dining area were decorated in keeping with the given season. Those attending the event could select a variety of food from one or all of the four seasons' tables. Each year the event grew larger and became so successful that it had to be moved from the church to the downtown Convention Center. Lorine served as President of District 1 for 20 years. During that time, when problems arose, she solved them with fairness and with respect for the views of the membership. She always prayed to God to help her to make the right decision for the organization. She led with compassion, wisdom, dignity and strength. A striking example of her lasting influence was seen after she stepped down as President and the organization ran into financial problems. Rather than seek redress by going to court, Lorine and others who were more senior members convinced the membership to settle the matter internally. She impressed upon the membership the Christian principles upon which the organization was founded and its existence for more than 100 years without a single encounter with the courts. Under the guidance of such principles, she steered the membership to believe in the presence and power of God in the situation and to leave such matters in the hands of God, the true Judge. In addition, she advised the membership to establish rules that in the future would provide the needed transparency in the handling of the organization's funds.

Lorine's last project before stepping down as President of District 1 was the erection of a tent hall on property adjacent to her home on Ellis Street. Her vision was for a facility large enough and adequately equipped to accommodate meetings, conferences, banquets and other activities for the Tent Chapter in the Fayetteville area and beyond. She motivated the membership to purchase the tract of land adjacent to her home, and construction of the facility began. However, because of cost overruns and other unexpected expenses, the organization experienced financial problems in completing the project. That did not discourage Lorine. The walls and foundation were completed, but the organization scarcely had enough money to put on the roof. Lorine prayed and looked for a contractor that would construct the roof at a reduced price. Her prayer was answered. The roofing contractor whom they found was a young man who was a novice in the construction business. During the roofing construction process, Lorine told him about the United Order of Tents, its purpose and its legacy. The contractor finished the roof ahead of time and then asked her if he could be contracted to finish the entire building project. Up to that time he had not told her that he also had a construction company. She, however, reminded him of the financial condition of the organization, but he told her not to worry about it but to just grant him permission to complete the building. She did and shortly afterward a fullfledged construction operation began.

The interior, plumbing, electrical, heating and air conditioning were all completed in a timely manner. Upon completing the interior, the contractor supplied a stove and refrigerator for the kitchen. He then moved to the parking lot which he paved and then landscaped the site. When he finished, Lorine asked him how much the organization owed him. She almost fainted when he said, "You owe me nothing." Lorine estimated that Mr. Paul Lauren and his construction company spent at least $50,000 to complete the conference facility.

The Lorine C. McLeod Tent Hall now proudly stands at 321 Bradford Avenue as a testament to the lifelong work and faithfulness of a true Christian lady who believes that the best way to serve God is through helping other persons. Now at the tender age of 92 years, and in the autumn of her life, she continues to serve as the President Emeritus of her local chapter and a faithful member of Lewis Chapel Missionary Baptist Church. Lorine offers the following advice to her Tent sisters:

Stick close to the organization's constitution and bylaws, keep the mission of the Tent fresh in mind as you plan your activities and execute your programs, always work for the greater good, continue to recruit and encourage younger women to join and become active in the organization; and when problems arise, as they surely will, ask God to be your guide and have enough faith to believe that He will give you the strength and wisdom to move whatever mountain that may stand in your way.

Others, Lord, yes others,
Let this my motto be,
Help me to live for others,
That I may live for Thee.
(Charles D. Meigs, *Lord, Help Me From Day to Day*)

References

"Our history." http://www.unitedorderoftents.org/heritage.html

"Our housing." "http://www.unitedorderoftents.org/programs.html

"Past presidents." http://www.unitedorderoftents.org/past_presidents.html

"Successful women bridging the past and upholding the future." *The Fayetteville Press* June 2011, p 6. http://www.fayettevillepress.com/images/TFP062011A06,pdf

www.ingramcontent.com/pod-product-compliance
Lightning Source LLC
Chambersburg PA
CBHW032031230426
43671CB00005B/281